THE
ANGER
FALLACY
WORKBOOK

**Practical Exercises for Overcoming
Irritation, Frustration and Anger**

Ross G Menzies and Steven Laurent

AUSTRALIANACADEMIC**PRESS**

Other books in this series:
The Anger Fallacy: Uncovering the Irrationality of the Angry Mindset

First published 2014
Australian Academic Press Group Pty. Ltd.
18 Victor Russell Drive
Samford Valley QLD 4520, Australia
www.australianacademicpress.com.au

ISBN: 9781922117373

Publisher: Stephen May

Copy Editor: Rhonda McPherson

Cover design: Emily Boldeman, Bird Project

Page design & typesetting: Australian Academic Press

Printing: Lightning Source

Contents

About the Authors

Associate Professor Ross G. Menzies has been providing cognitive–behaviour therapy for anxiety, depression, anger, couples conflict and related issues for over two decades. He completed a B.Sc (Psych), M.Psychol (Clin), and a PhD in clinical psychology at the University of New South Wales in Sydney, Australia. He is currently Associate Professor in Health Sciences at the University of Sydney. He is the past New South Wales' president, and twice national president, of the Australian Association for Cognitive Behaviour Therapy (AACBT). He is the long-standing editor of Australia's national CBT scientific journal, Behaviour Change. He has recently been appointed the convenor and president of the 8th World Congress of Behavioural and Cognitive Therapies to be held in Australia in 2016.

Associate Professor Menzies is an active researcher and currently holds over $5 million in national competitive research grants. He has produced 5 books, over 150 international journal manuscripts and book chapters and is regularly invited to speak at conferences and leading universities and institutions around the world. He continues to attract patients from across metropolitan Sydney, rural New South Wales, interstate and from overseas, with many individuals and families travelling thousands of kilometres to receive treatment at his private practice. The current book is his second major work on anger.

Steven Laurent is a clinical psychologist with extensive experience in treating the full range of psychiatric disorders. He is regular guest lecturer at the University of Sydney, where he has taught on anger-related disorders and states, mood disorders, anxiety disorders, and drug and alcohol disorders. Currently, he works in private practice in the inner west of Sydney. Laurent completed a masters in Clinical Psychology at the University of New South Wales, where his thesis centred on facial perception in 'psychopaths'. Laurent's interest in anger arose in the 1990s during the completion of undergraduate degrees in philosophy and formal logic at the Sorbonne in Paris.

Acknowledgements

To my great loves — Margot, Rachel, Henry, Matilda, and Jude.
And, once again, in memory of my great guide, J. Christopher Clarke.
— R.G.M.

To my ever-loving mum — thanks for bailing me out, once again …
— S.L.

Preface

We wrote our original volume, *The Anger Fallacy*, with two firm convictions:

1. For our arguments and insights to stick, we were going to need tasks that forced the reader to really engage with and process the material.

2. Most readers won't be bothered to actually do such tasks.

This placed us in a bind.

What we decided to do was scatter short, simple exercises and thought experiments throughout the book in such a way that if the breezier among you even *glanced* at them, they might still do the trick. Our initial test data now support this claim. That is, simply reading *The Anger Fallacy* has been shown to significantly reduce scores on formal self-report tests of anger. For the keener among you, however, who want to take this work further, we have now produced this supplementary volume of more interactive and experiential tasks. The pedagogy is sound: the deeper and more actively you process information the better you learn it and recall it. These tasks, if you actually do them, will deepen and consolidate your thinking on anger by transforming you from passive reader to active thinker.

Before attempting these exercises, however, you really need to read *The Anger Fallacy* from cover to cover at least once. Many of the exercises (though not all) rest on assumed knowledge from the original book.

We hope you will enjoy these exercises as you progress in your mastery over anger, the darkest of all emotions.

Ross G. Menzies and Steven Laurent

Anger Monitoring

OK, let's get going! If it's a long time since you've read *The Anger Fallacy*, we suggest you have a quick re-read. As we emphasised in the preface, the exercises in this workbook are meant to supplement and extend the work you began with the original volume.

Now let's begin with some simple monitoring. Over the coming months, as you complete this workbook, record all situations in which you feel anger in the included monitoring sheet(s) that are your Anger Diary. In this way, you will have a clear record of the frequency and intensity of your anger, and also the situations in which it occurs. You'll be tracking these variables just as you might track your weight over time if you were following a diet, or your lap time if you were learning to swim.

We expect you'll find that with time and effort you will get angry less often, and less intensely. Some situations that annoyed you at the start will no longer annoy you at all; others that would usually put you in a rage will only mildly irritate you; and certain incidents that might otherwise have left you brooding for hours may only bother you for minutes or seconds. You will never attain zero anger; though it's certainly possible to aspire to zero anger.

Most of the monitoring sheet is relatively self-explanatory, but just a word or two on the EVENT column, and the THOUGHTS column. Many of our clients tend to blur these categories, mostly without realising it. The EVENT column is designed to be a very dry and objective description of the situation that gave rise to your anger — the bare facts of what happened. Be wary not to inject evaluations or interpretations into this section. So, for example, you are to write: 'Email from my boss stating that there had been a complaint lodged against me'. Not: 'My idiot boss wrote an insulting email basically accusing me of being a loose cannon'." (You can write, 'My boss is an idiot; his email was insulting; he was basically accusing me of being a loose cannon' in THOUGHTS). Similarly, in the EVENT column write: 'My wife shushed me when I asked her where the remote was'. Not: 'My wife was rude and disrespectful'.

	Date	Event or Situation	Thoughts or Images	Degree of Anger (Out of 100)	Behaviour
ⓘ	25/1/14	At home with children, who won't tidy their room.	They should clean up this bloody mess — and do as they're told!	40	Scolded them, yelled, refused to let them see the afternoon movie; wasted the afternoon carrying on …

Date	Event or Situation	Thoughts or Images	Degree of Anger (Out of 100)	Behaviour
25/1/14	At home with children, who won't tidy their room.	They should clean up this bloody mess — and do as they're told!	40	Scolded them, yelled, refused to let them see the afternoon movie; wasted the afternoon carrying on ...

	Date	Event or Situation	Thoughts or Images	Degree of Anger (Out of 100)	Behaviour
ⓘ	25/1/14	At home with children, who won't tidy their room.	They should clean up this bloody mess — and do as they're told!	40	Scolded them, yelled, refused to let them see the afternoon movie; wasted the afternoon carrying on …

Date	Event or Situation	Thoughts or Images	Degree of Anger (Out of 100)	Behaviour
25/1/14	At home with children, who won't tidy their room.	They should clean up this bloody mess — and do as they're told!	40	Scolded them, yelled, refused to let them see the afternoon movie; wasted the afternoon carrying on …

Date	Event or Situation	Thoughts or Images	Degree of Anger (Out of 100)	Behaviour
25/1/14	At home with children, who won't tidy their room.	They should clean up this bloody mess — and do as they're told!	40	Scolded them, yelled, refused to let them see the afternoon movie; wasted the afternoon carrying on …

ⓘ

Identifying 'Shoulds'

As you learned in the early chapters of *The Anger Fallacy*, anger is associated with individualised rules or 'shoulds' that you carry around with you. In the following examples, write the 'should' that you believe best accounts for the anger experienced in the scene.

Example 1 Rob has been standing at the counter in the cheese shop for five minutes. The shop assistant has been gossiping on the phone to a friend. Rob is angry.

What is Rob thinking?

ⓘ The shop assistant SHOULD get off the phone and serve me.

Example 2 Mary is waiting for her friend Kate at the movies. Mary has sent a text message to Kate who is now 10 minutes late. Mary wrote: "Are you far away?". Five minutes has passed and Kate hasn't responded. Mary is angry.

What is Mary thinking?

_____ SHOULD _____

Example 3 Peter's wife has asked him to mow the lawn while he is watching a basketball game on the television. Peter is angry.

What is Peter thinking?

_____ SHOULD _____

Example 4 George's new phone won't fit in any of the docking stations in his house. George is angry.

What is George thinking?

_____ SHOULD _____

Example 5 Tony is driving fast. He is in a hurry to make it to work on time. The driver in front of him is driving 5 km/h below the speed limit, which is slowing Tony's trip down. He is very angry.

What is Tony thinking?

_____ SHOULD _____

Example 6 Claire's computer has crashed while she was writing an important university essay. She had not backed up her work. Claire is angry.

What is Claire thinking?

_____ SHOULD _____

Example 7 Mario has asked Julia out on a date. She thanked him, but said she 'didn't like him in that way'. Mario is angry.

What is Mario thinking?

_____ SHOULD _____

Finding Alternatives to 'Shoulds'

In the following scenes, we want you first to write a 'should' thought that could have caused the anger. Then write two alternative statements that could have led to more adaptive or helpful responses by the central character. These exercises will help you to see that there are many alternatives to anger.

Example | You are sitting down at home to watch a movie, when an electrical blackout occurs. You ring the emergency information line and they tell you that the power will be out for two hours. You are angry.

What is the thought that is driving your anger?

ⓘ Electrical blackouts SHOULD not occur when I'm about to watch a movie.

Can you think of alternative ways that you could have thought in this scene? Write two alternative thoughts that might have saved the night by not causing anger.

ⓘ Alternative: I could do with an early night. This is a good excuse

ⓘ Alternative: These things are nobody's fault. I'm not the only one affected here — there could be someone needing my help ... ?

ⓘ Alternative: Lucky I have my ipad charged!

ⓘ Alternative: This will give us all a chance to talk. We always sit in front of screens

ⓘ Alternative: Let's go out for ice-cream

Example 2 You suggest a restaurant to your friends that you really like. After some email discussion, the dominant member of your group convinces everyone that their choice might be even better. You are angry.

What is the thought that is driving your anger?

_____ SHOULD _____

Can you think of alternative ways that you could have thought in this situation?

Alternative 1: _____

Alternative 2: _____

Example 3 Your babysitter calls you to let you know that she is sick, and won't be able to work for you tonight. You will have to cancel your dinner plans and you are angry.

What is the thought that is driving your anger?

_____ SHOULD _____

Can you think of alternative ways that you could have thought in this situation?

Alternative 1: _____

Alternative 2: _____

Example 4 You have been given a speeding ticket at the bottom of a steep decline. You complain to the police officer about the placement of the speed camera, arguing that it took advantage of the speed that was gained travelling down the steep slope. The officer smiles and continues to write you a ticket. You are angry.

What is the thought that is driving your anger?

_____ SHOULD _____

Can you think of alternative ways that you could have thought in this situation?

Alternative 1: _____

Alternative 2: _____

Example 5 You hand in your university assignment 5 minutes late. You are informed that, as your handbook states, the penalty is a 10% deduction in marks. You comment on the unfairness of such a penalty for only 5 minutes delay. You are angry.

What is the thought that is driving your anger?

_____ SHOULD _____

Can you think of alternative ways that you could have thought in this situation?

Alternative 1: _____

Alternative 2: _____

Example 6 You take a book back to your local bookstore and ask for a refund. They refuse, saying that the cover is now bent and that you have damaged the book. You are angry.

What is the thought that is driving your anger?

_____ SHOULD _____

Can you think of alternative ways that you could have thought in this situation?

Alternative 1: _____

Alternative 2: _____

Example 7 You are discussing the history of interest rates at a dinner party. Someone is incorrectly stating the 'facts', claiming that your favourite leader presided over record high rates. Despite knowing that your friend is wrong, you cannot convince them and they won't budge from their position. You are angry.

What is the thought that is driving your anger?

_____ SHOULD _____

Can you think of alternative ways that you could have thought in this situation?

Alternative 1: _____

Alternative 2: _____

Example 8 Your mother is asking you whether you think it's 'time to settle down'. She criticises you for 'letting your last girlfriend get away'. You are angry.

What is the thought that is driving your anger?

_____ SHOULD _____

Can you think of alternative ways that you could have thought in this situation?

Alternative 1: _____

Alternative 2: _____

Example 9 You have two children attending an expensive private school. To your shock, they inform you that there is no place for your third child when you seek to enrol him. They tell you that all places are currently taken by other children. You are angry.

What is the thought that is driving your anger?

_____ SHOULD _____

Can you think of alternative ways that you could have thought in this situation?

Alternative 1: _____

Alternative 2: _____

Example 10 The person seated next to you on the plane is very overweight. Their body rests against yours and you are facing a 14-hour flight. You are angry.

What is the thought that is driving your anger?

_____ SHOULD _____

Can you think of alternative ways that you could have thought in this situation?

Alternative 1: _____

Alternative 2: _____

Recognising the Arbitrariness and Silliness of Anger

To complete this exercise you must first watch Episode 21 of Series 3 of the television series *Seinfeld*. The episode, 'The Parking Space', centres on a fight between George and another driver over a space in the front of Jerry's building. As you will see, the standoff continues for many hours and the whole neighbourhood joins in. After you have watched the episode, complete the following questions:

Question 1 Before the confrontation, Elaine suggests to George that they park Jerry's car in a parking garage. Why does George refuse?

_____

_____

_____

Question 2 How does the argument between George and Mike begin?

_____

_____

_____

Question 3 When each driver refuses to move his car, what happens?

_____

_____

_____

Question 4 Mike tells George, 'you're not getting that space!'. He continues, 'I'll sleep in my car if I have to!'. How does George respond? What does he say? What does this teach you about the nature of anger?

_____

_____

_____

Question 5 How do they handle the situation when the ice-cream truck needs to get around the two cars?

_____

_____

_____

Question 6 Do any of the characters from the episode get to see the boxing match at Jerry's that they came to watch?

_____

_____

Question 7 Did they get to do anything fun from the moment the argument begins?

_____

Question 8 How long does the argument continue?

Question 9 Do you think the parking space was worth the cost of the argument? Was the dispute over parking really worth all they went through to win the space?

Question 10 Have you ever behaved like this over something trivial? Describe a similar example of anger from your own life.

Question 11 Initially, Kramer defends Mike over pulling into the space. Did anything happen earlier in the episode that might have influenced Kramer's opinion?

_____

_____

Question 12 Initially, Jerry seems convinced that George is right. Did anything happen earlier in the episode that might have influenced Jerry's opinion?

_____

_____

_____

Question 13 Everyone seems to have a strong view about who is right in this argument. Why do you think everyone holds their own opinions so strongly?

_____

_____

_____

Question 14 List three things about anger that you have learned from this exercise.

1._____

2._____

3._____

Finding Humour

There's actually a fine line between anger and humour. When you think about it, the scenes in which we're angry are often the same scenes that we would laugh at in comedies. When they happen to *us*, we get angry, yet we can easily see the funny side of the same events when they happen to other people, or when we think about them later. In many ways, humour and anger are close cousins.

If you'd rather laugh at minor annoyances than get too upset by them, watch the film *Planes, Trains and Automobiles*. Steven Martin's character is subjected to 1001 annoyances, mostly at the hands of the likeable but infuriating character played by John Candy. What is the difference between finding these things funny or annoying? Recall a time you got angry in a Planes, Trains and Automobiles-type situation and describe it in the following space.

_____

_____

_____

_____

_____

Can you laugh at this scene, now? What has changed?

_____

_____

_____

_____

The central characters of our favourite television comedy (you'll never guess which) cannot find their car in a shopping centre car park (see also Exercise 14). They walk about for hours from one level to the next in a fruitless search.

How would you normally react in a scene like this?

_____

_____

_____

Can you see the funny side of this scene?   YES/NO

How would you like to react in scenes like this in the future?

_____

_____

_____

What do you think are the advantages of finding humour in life's difficult situations?

_____

_____

_____

How would others react to the two alternative versions of you? Do you think your friends and family would have more respect for your old 'angry' reactions or your new 'humour-based' reactions to life's uncomfortable moments? Think about this carefully and discuss below.

_____

_____

_____

_____

_____

Mea Culpa
— Apologising for Your Anger

Sometimes people get stuck in anger because they find it hard to apologise for their outbursts. Rather than saying sorry, they find it easier to dig their heels in and stay angry. They refuse to admit their own failings, not wanting to lose face or back down. Choose five scenes in which you have been angry in the past 12 months and write an apology for your behaviour. You don't have to actually send your apology, but you may choose to if you wish.

In your apology (1) make a clear statement taking responsibility for your behaviour; (2) don't rationalise (i.e., don't try to blame other people for the way you acted); and (3) explain the fault in your thinking that led to your reaction. That is, identify the 'should'.

If you're lacking inspiration, you might want to re-read W. Livingston Larned's moving apology to his son on page 10 of *The Anger Fallacy*.

Apology I

_____

_____

_____

_____

Apology 2

_____

_____

_____

_____

Apology 3

_____

_____

_____

_____

Apology 4

_____

_____

_____

_____

Apology 5

_____

_____

_____

_____

Explaining the Origin of Your 'Shoulds'

As you learned in *The Anger Fallacy*, your 'shoulds' are simply the product of your learning history. That is, your beliefs are not inherently correct — they are no more correct than your neighbours' equal and opposite beliefs! From your early childhood you have been learning from the environment around you — from your parents, grandparents, siblings, teachers, friends, books, songs, movies, television and so on. In this exercise, we want you to practice tracing the origin of your 'shoulds'. It will help you see how arbitrary they are. First, pick a 'should' from the supplied list that you think is a part of your beliefs or attitudes. Then, list all the early influences in your life that you believe may have implanted that rule into your belief system.

Pick a 'should' from the following list that you currently believe to be true:

- Parents should put the needs of their children first.
- Every child should get a university education.
- People should wait their turn and not jump places in queues.
- People should return an email within a day of receiving it.
- People should keep regular contact with their parents.
- You should call if you are going to be late home.
- People should be on time when they are meeting friends.
- Everyone should support their friends.
- Couples should sort out any disputes they are having before they sleep.

- A woman should take on the man's surname when she marries.
- People should treat me as they would have me treat them.
- Others should treat me as I treat them.
- You should never lend money to friends..

Which 'should' did you choose?

_____

_____

List all of the influences that you think played a role in you forming this 'should'. That is, describe all of the factors that may have helped you form this belief. Think about the influence of your parents, friends, siblings, television and so on.

_____

_____

_____

_____

_____

Now pick another 'should' (not necessarily from the list) that you believe.

_____

_____

Once again, list all the influences and factors that have influenced the formation of your 'should'.

_____

_____

_____

_____

_____

And let's do one more. Which 'should' did you choose?

_____

Again, list the influences that formed this 'should' in your mind.

_____

_____

_____

_____

_____

Clearly, your 'shoulds' are simply the result of influences around you in your learning history. In this sense, they are arbitrary — a random product of your biography. That is, if you had a different learning history you would have acquired different 'shoulds'. Every one of the 7 billion people on the planet has had a subtly different learning history. Hence, they will have subtly different 'shoulds'.

Explaining the Origin of Someone Else's Shoulds

Just as it can be useful to understand the origins of your own 'shoulds', you will be helped in your interpersonal relationships by understanding the 'shoulding' of those around you. For this exercise, we want you to trace the origin of a 'should' that appears to be held by someone you love. Make sure you pick someone that you know well, a close friend, a sibling or perhaps your partner — it will make it easier to identify the influences that were involved in the development of the 'should'. You might want to discuss this exercise with the person you have chosen. It might help you to identify influences previously unknown to you. Remember, empathy is one solution to anger (see chapter 10, *The Anger Fallacy*).

Pick a 'should' from the following list that is held by someone close to you:

- Parents should put the needs of their children first.
- Every child should get a university education.
- People should wait their turn and not jump places in queues.
- People should return an email within a day of receiving it.
- People should keep regular contact with their parents.
- You should call if you are going to be late home.
- People should be on time when they are meeting friends.
- Everyone should support their friends.

- Couples should sort out any disputes they are having before they sleep.
- A woman should take on the man's surname when she marries.
- People should treat me as they would have me treat them.
- Others should treat me as I treat them.
- You should never lend money to friends.

Which 'should' did you choose?

_____

List all of the influences that you think played a role in forming this 'should' in your loved one. That is, describe all of the factors that may have helped them form this belief. Think about the influence of their parents, friends, siblings, milieu and so on.

_____

_____

_____

_____

Now pick another 'should' (not necessarily from the list) that you know this individual endorses.

_____

Once again, list all the influences and factors that have influenced the formation of their 'should'.

_____

_____

_____

_____

And let's do one more.

Which 'should' did you choose?

Again, list the influences that formed this 'should' in their mind.

Clearly, just like your own, the 'shoulds' of your loved ones and friends are simply the result of their learning history. Once again, it is clear that 'shoulds' are arbitrary constructions of the human mind.

Cultivating Gratitude

As modern day westerners, accustomed to a certain standard of living, we often forget how lucky we are. We do a lot of complaining about First World problems, and very little praising, appreciating or relishing of 'First World solutions'. We focus on the minor things that are going wrong, rather than the major things that are going right. In the following exercises, you are asked to explore the good fortune that you regularly experience by living in a modern western society (see further pages 232–234 of *The Anger Fallacy*).

Ever been peeved at the time it took for your coffee to arrive? Or at the service you received in the cafe? Let's explore the large number of people that might be involved in bringing you your coffee. See if you can find out the actual number of people involved in various parts of this process. Taking the trouble answer the following questions could be quite enlightening.

1. How many people are employed by the Vittoria worldwide?

   _____

2. How many people are employed by Saeco, the Italian company that makes the coffee machine?

   _____

3. Contact your local milk supplier. How many staff do they employ, including the drivers that deliver the milk?

   _____

4. Contact your local supplier of insulated disposable cups. How many staff do they employ?

    _____

5. Vittoria source beans from Brazil. How many people are employed in the agriculture of the coffee beans in Brazil?

    _____

6. How many people are involved in the barista training program that the staff have completed at your cafe?

    _____

7. Oh, and don't forget to count the barista and wait staff at the café.

    _____

Your coffee costs a few bucks but is the product of thousands of people's efforts around the globe. The answers you've found to the earlier questions only scratch the surface. (We have not included the shipbuilders, metal miners, and many others that are involved in transporting the beans.) Do you think 5 or 10 minutes is too long to wait? How do you think you should respond to a few minutes' delay? Is a sense of injustice really warranted in the scene?

_____

_____

_____

_____

_____

Do you ever get angry in these types of situations? Do you forget to focus on how fortunate you are in everyday situations?

Below list five examples of forgetting to focus on the positives. If you can't think of five 'cappuccino' moments simply list as many as you can. You can always come back and complete the rest of the exercise as they pop into your mind over time.

Focusing on the Positives

Example 1

_____

_____

_____

_____

Example 2

_____

_____

_____

_____

Example 3

_____

_____

_____

_____

Example 4

_____

_____

_____

_____

_____

Example 5

_____

_____

_____

_____

_____

Overcoming the Need for Fairness

'Fairness shoulds' are so common that we dedicated an entire chapter to them in *The Anger Fallacy* (see chapter 11). From early childhood, people commonly display anger if they think the world is treating them unfairly. 'He's already had two biscuits (or some such thing) and I've only had one' is a common complaint of the young in most households. In this exercise, we want to turn your attention to unfairness *in your favour*. Think of 3 situations in the past in which YOU have had an unfair advantage or undeserved luck. That is, think of three times that YOU have had the 'good break', 'good fortune' or 'good luck'. The world is not fair, but explore how YOU have benefited from that fact. Consider the plight of the impoverished members of the global community as you complete this exercise.

Example

I have had unfair access to a first-class medical system at critical points in my life. When I was rushed to hospital with severe chest pain I was ushered straight through emergency, tested immediately with bloods, scans and various forms of monitoring. I know that for many individuals this simply wouldn't have happened. I know that many people simply die in these situations.

Situation I

_____

_____

_____

_____

_____

Situation 2

_____

_____

_____

_____

_____

Situation 3

_____

_____

_____

_____

_____

The average person on the planet lives on less than $3 per day, with limited access to clean water, fresh fruit, meat and vegetables. Do you think this is fair? Do you really think you have reason to get angry when someone jumps the queue at your delicatessen? In the scheme of things, don't you think that the world has treated you unfairly well? Discuss.

_____

_____

_____

_____

_____

_____

_____

What Went Well Today?

As discussed earlier, anger often occurs because individuals are focusing on the minor negatives of the day, rather than the positives that are occurring all around them. For the next 30 days we want you to record three things that went well each day, and what made them special.

Example 1

My drive to work went well, because the local roads authority has skilfully managed the roads and traffic lights to move a million drivers each day through the city.

Example 2

My evening pasta was delicious because my local shop has excellent canned tomatoes from northern Italy, pasta from South Australia, fresh herbs from Sydney, Parmesan cheese from Reggiano, and extra virgin olive oil from Spain.

Example 3

I taught a good English class today, because of my enthusiasm and talent as a teacher and the excellent training I received at a modern university.

Example 4

My photograph of George Harrison arrived for only $45 because of a world-wide on-line auction network that gives me access to hundreds of thousands of items around the globe that are only a few key-strokes away.

Record What Went Well

Record your three items each day for 30 days of what went well. And yes, we do mean *every* day. We really believe that this process will help you change. Of course, you may wish to continue with other exercises in the book across these 30 days.

Day 1. Date _____

(a) _____

_____

(b) _____

_____

(c) _____

_____

Day 2. Date _____

(a) _____

_____

(b) _____

_____

(c) _____

_____

Day 3. Date _____

(a) _____

_____

(b) _____

_____

(c) _____

_____

Day 4. Date _____

(a) _____

_____

(b) _____

_____

(c) _____

_____

Day 5. Date _____

(a) _____

_____

(b) _____

_____

(c) _____

_____

Day 6. Date _____

(a) _____

_____

(b) _____

_____

(c) _____

_____

Day 7. Date _____

(a) _____

_____

(b) _____

_____

(c) _____

_____

Day 8. Date _____

(a) _____

_____

(b) _____

_____

(c) _____

_____

Day 9. Date _____

    (a) _____

       _____

    (b) _____

       _____

    (c) _____

       _____

Day 10. Date _____

    (a) _____

       _____

    (b) _____

       _____

    (c) _____

       _____

Day 11. Date _____

    (a) _____

       _____

    (b) _____

       _____

    (c) _____

_____

Day 12. Date _____

    (a) _____

    _____

    (b) _____

    _____

    (c) _____

    _____

Day 13. Date _____

    (a) _____

    _____

    (b) _____

    _____

    (c) _____

    _____

Day 14. Date _____

    (a) _____

    _____

    (b) _____

    _____

(c) _____

_____

Day 15. Date _____

(a) _____

_____

(b) _____

_____

(c) _____

_____

Day 16. Date _____

(a) _____

_____

(b) _____

_____

(c) _____

_____

Day 17. Date _____

(a) _____

_____

(b) _____

_____

(c) _____

_____

Day 18. Date _____

(a) _____

_____

(b) _____

_____

(c) _____

_____

Day 19. Date _____

(a) _____

_____

(b) _____

_____

(c) _____

_____

Day 20. Date _____

(a) _____

_____

(b) _____

_____

(c) _____

_____

Day 21. Date _____

(a) _____

_____

(b) _____

_____

(c) _____

_____

Day 22. Date _____

(a) _____

_____

(b) _____

_____

(c) _____

_____

Day 23. Date _____

(a) _____

_____

(b)_____

_____

(c)_____

_____

Day 24. Date _____

(a) _____

_____

(b)_____

_____

(c)_____

_____

Day 25. Date _____

(a) _____

_____

(b)_____

_____

(c)_____

_____

Day 26. Date _____

    (a) _____

        _____

    (b) _____

        _____

    (c) _____

        _____

Day 27. Date _____

    (a) _____

        _____

    (b) _____

        _____

    (c) _____

        _____

Day 28. Date _____

    (a) _____

        _____

    (b) _____

        _____

(c) _____

_____

Day 29. Date _____

(a) _____

_____

(b) _____

_____

(c) _____

_____

Day 30. Date _____

(a) _____

_____

(b) _____

_____

(c) _____

_____

Identify the Costs of Your Anger

Angry people often tell us about how anger has worked for them on some occasions. They are convinced that anger has delivered some gains in their life. In this exercise, we want you to face the *costs* of your anger. These costs are often overlooked or minimised by the angry. We want you to list all of the negative effects that anger has had on your life. We want you to list the potentially wonderful moments that have been lost because of your anger. The following example is the response from Paul, a 43-year-old angry accountant:

> Anger cost me my first marriage. I expected my wife to just follow my rules and meet my expectations. I was an idiot. I was inflexible and rule-bound. I ruined so many wonderful nights — I killed so many holidays and evenings out. My anger, mostly about trivial and stupid things, led me to cancel so many outings and lose so many opportunities. I realise now that I can never get those moments back. I have lost them. I have lost all those moments over my own ridiculous sense of self-importance. I left two jobs because I couldn't get along with my co-workers, and even stopped watching football because of my constant frustration with referees!! I don't talk to my sister and have lost several friends over stupid disagreements. My anger has never really helped me. It has only created pain and suffering. I wish I had known it all much earlier in my life.

What are the costs of *your* anger?

_____

_____

_____

_____

_____

_____

_____

_____

_____

_____

Identifying How Anger Interferes With Problem-Solving in Real Situations

Often we forget how many alternatives to anger there are when dealing with everyday problems. You could have written an email to the Telstra complaints department, rather than screaming at the support staff on the phone. You could have simply returned the chipped cup after opening the box rather than throwing it against the wall. Choose five angry events from your past and explain how you could have dealt with them without anger. Why would the outcomes have been better without the anger you felt? How did anger interfere with simply solving the problem at hand?

Record Five Events

Event 1 Describe an angry event from your past.

_____

_____

What did you do in this situation? How did you display your anger?

_____

_____

How did this interfere with simply solving the problem at hand?

_____

_____

What could you have done, without anger, to better deal with the problem?

_____

_____

Event 2 Describe an angry event from your past.

_____

_____

What did you do in this situation? How did you display your anger?

_____

_____

How did this interfere with simply solving the problem at hand?

_____

_____

What could you have done, without anger, to better deal with the problem?

_____

_____

Event 3 Describe an angry event from your past.

_____

_____

What did you do in this situation? How did you display your anger?

_____

_____

How did this interfere with simply solving the problem at hand?

_____

_____

What could you have done, without anger, to better deal with the problem?

_____

_____

Event 4 Describe an angry event from your past.

_____

_____

What did you do in this situation? How did you display your anger?

_____

_____

How did this interfere with simply solving the problem at hand?

_____

_____

What could you have done, without anger, to better deal with the problem?

_____

_____

Event 5 Describe an angry event from your past.

_____

_____

What did you do in this situation? How did you display your anger?

_____

_____

How did this interfere with simply solving the problem at hand?

_____

_____

What could you have done, without anger, to better deal with the problem?

_____

_____

Nonuniversality of Ethics — Differences in Law

People sometimes say to us, 'but surely laws are "right" — surely it's OK to *should* about laws'?

Well here's a brief assignment to bring home how historically and culturally determined laws really are.

Research any *changes* in the laws regarding any of the following issues within your own country over the last century (choose one):

- age of consent for sex
- domestic violence
- animal cruelty
- homosexuality
- euthanasia
- age for legal drinking
- advertising of tobacco products
- management of endangered species.

Have there been changes in the way your community views these issues? Have the laws changed? What does this tell you about the law? Is it an arbitrary construction of a particular community at a particular time?

_____

_____

_____

_____

_____

_____

_____

_____

_____

Now research current differences between laws in your country and those in three other countries from the following list (choose one, but not the same one as in the previous exercise):

- age of consent for sex
- domestic violence
- animal cruelty
- homosexuality
- euthanasia
- age for legal drinking
- advertising of tobacco products
- management of endangered species.

Are there differences between communities in the handling of these issues? Again, what does this tell you about the arbitrariness of laws?

_____

_____

_____

_____

_____

_____

_____

_____

_____

Have you previously thought that your community's current laws are 'right' or 'correct'? On reflection, do you agree that behaviours are neither 'right' nor 'wrong'? Can you see that whether a behaviour is viewed as acceptable or not depends on when (in history) you ask the question, and who you ask?

_____

_____

_____

_____

_____

_____

_____

Given what you have discovered in this exercise, do you think anger is warranted toward people who hold different views to your own?

NOTE WELL

The ideas covered in this exercise (and the next) are quite challenging and we particularly encourage you to re-read two chapters in *The Anger Fallacy* — chapter 8, 'The arbitrariness of shoulds' and chapter 9, 'Seeing the machine' — if you are finding them tricky. But we do want to make a few points clear.

- We are NOT saying that laws should be abolished.
- We are NOT denying that some behaviours hurt people.
- We are NOT denying that some behaviours are more helpful to the individual and the functioning of a community than others.
- We AGREE that controls over the behaviour of individuals (i.e., laws) help the smooth functioning of communities.

- And, we are NOT against individuals seeking to influence the views of others in trying to build safer communities.

So what are we saying? Put simply, we are suggesting that anger toward those with different views is misguided and irrational. Believing that you hold all the adaptive, helpful or 'correct' views on human behaviour is arrogant and foolish.

Nonuniversality of Ethics
— the Case of Killing

After completing the last exercise many readers complain that there are still *some* universal ethics. They plead that some behaviours are regarded as wrong by all. Some argue that 'to kill' is consistently seen as wrong across time, cultural divides and individual differences. Let's test this thesis out. Answer the following questions by circling one of the choices provided.

- Is it wrong to kill a person? YES/NO/DEPENDS
- What if you're wearing an army uniform and he is your opponent in war? Is it wrong? YES/NO/DEPENDS
- Is it wrong to kill a serial rapist (i.e., are you against the death penalty for such a criminal)? YES/NO/DEPENDS
- Is it wrong to kill a serial killer (i.e., are you against the death penalty for such a criminal? YES/NO/DEPENDS
- Is it wrong to kill a whale for food? YES/NO/DEPENDS
- Is it wrong to kill a cow for food? YES/NO/DEPENDS
- Is it wrong to kill a mosquito? YES/NO/DEPENDS
- Is it wrong to kill a plant? YES/NO/DEPENDS
- Is it wrong to kill an unborn foetus before 10 weeks gestation (i.e., are you against abortion)? YES/NO/DEPENDS

- What if the foetus has significant health problems that will make for a difficult and disabled life? Is it wrong? YES/NO/DEPENDS

- Is it wrong for the elderly to kill themselves even if they're terminally ill and strongly wish to die? YES/NO/DEPENDS

- Is it wrong to assist the elderly in killing themselves even if they're terminally ill and strongly wish to die? YES/NO/DEPENDS

Now ask at least half a dozen of your friends or associates the same questions. Ideally, choose individuals who represent different cultural backgrounds as well as varying age and gender. Did they all give the same answers? Did everyone say 'yes' to all of these questions? If not, do you agree that even something as fundamental as killing depends on an individual's perspective arising from their particular learning history? Write about the influences on your answers. List all the early influences in your life that you believe may have created your belief system on killing:

_____

_____

_____

_____

_____

Given what you have discovered in this exercise, do you really think anger is warranted toward people who hold different views to you?

_____

_____

_____

_____

_____

The Ugliness of Other People's Anger

As we explored in chapter 3 of *The Anger Fallacy*, anger can be an ugly emotion. In the main, angry people look pathetic, out of control, nasty or sulky. The angry can go red in the face; their nostrils may flare. They may start to stutter and lose their voice as they yell. People around the angry individual are usually embarrassed — tending to make apologetic faces at passers by. Of course, not every angry person is a screamer. Some just sit silently, like sulking brattish children.

Think about your most recent experiences of other people's anger. We want you to record honestly how others have looked to you when they have been angry. Have you winced as you watched? Have you ever laughed at them? Did they look pathetic or childish to you? How did others respond to them? Do you see them as strong or weak?

Record your last three experiences of other people's anger.

Experience 1

_____

_____

_____

_____

Experience 2

_____

_____

_____

_____

_____

Experience 3

_____

_____

_____

_____

The Ugliness of Your Own Anger

Have you ever thought about how *you* appear when you're angry? Have you ever heard yourself screaming, or thought about what your sulking or brooding must look like? Chances are, red is not your most flattering colour. We want you to get a glimpse of what you look and sound like in these scenes. Ideally, find or obtain actual footage of yourself (genuinely) angry; alternatively, just film yourself replaying a recent angry scene. If you don't have access to a camera or smart phone, you can act it out in front of a mirror. Don't hold back — try to relive the excesses of your behaviour in the scene. Watch your face (whether you're a screamer or a sulker), and imagine that you are on the receiving end, or a witness to the scene.

Describe what you saw.

_____

_____

_____

Does it remind you of anyone?

_____

_____

_____

How do think the receiver would have felt in the scene described?

_____

_____

_____

What do you think these scenes do to your relationships with loved ones?

_____

_____

_____

How would you like to be in the future in these scenes? Describe the sort of person you would like to become in dealing with the everyday difficulties of life.

_____

_____

_____

Anger in Situations Beyond Your Control

To complete this exercise you must firstly watch episode 6 of series 3 of the television series *Seinfeld*. The episode, 'The Parking Garage', involves the central characters desperately searching for Kramer's car in a shopping mall parking lot. We get to compare and contrast how the different characters cope in this everyday situation. After you have watched the episode, complete the following questions.

How does George react when he first realises that Kramer doesn't know where they parked?

_____

_____

_____

George, in reference to recording the location of a car when you park, mutters under his breath, "You get into a parking lot, you write it down. How hard is that?"

He appears to be personally blaming Kramer. Why?

_____

_____

Jerry starts to complain about the lack of bathrooms in the shopping centre. "Don't they consult a urologist when they build one of these places", he says angrily. Is there any point to his anger? Will it achieve anything in the scene?

Jerry gets annoyed with Kramer, telling him, "from now on no more calling out 'I found it' unless we're sitting in it, OK?" Again, is there any point to this anger? Will it really achieve anything?

Elaine reacts with increasing anger toward those who won't drive her around the parking lot to look for the car. She yells at them and taunts them, and becomes verbally abusive. Does her anger help in these scenes? Does it achieve anything for Elaine or the group?

Jerry gets caught urinating behind a car. He blames Kramer because it was Kramer who suggested that he 'shouldn't hold it in'. Do you think it was Kramer's fault? Does blaming him help in any way?

_____

"Unbelievable", says George. "I'm never gonna get out of here". George is frustrated, but is his assessment of their situation too negative?

_____

_____

_____

George gets angry that the Mercedes has parked across two spaces. Again, is there any point to his anger, or is he fussing about something beyond his control? Does it achieve anything?

_____

_____

_____

Do you think there is ever a point to getting angry about things you can't control?

_____

_____

_____

Have you ever lost your car in a shopping centre car park? How did you react? Did you get angry? Did your anger help you in the scene?

_____

_____

_____

Most of the characters in this episode get angry and frustrated. They abuse each other, and their fellow shoppers. Did any of this help them find the car, or did anger get in the way of simply solving the problem? What do you think they should have done in this situation?

_____

_____

_____

George expresses a concern about dying. Kramer says he's not worried about death. In fact, Kramer is the only character in the episode who stays quite calm throughout. What does he say is the secret to life?

_____

_____

_____

List three things about anger that you have learned from this exercise.

1. _____

2. _____

3. _____

Your Own Anger in Situations Beyond Your Control

Some of the most ridiculous situations in which anger commonly arises are those that involve outcomes that are beyond your control. The furniture store has delivered the wrong lamp. The traffic is blocking your progress. Your computer has crashed. In each of these situations, the negative outcome has already occurred when you begin to experience anger. Therefore, your anger is completely pointless. It cannot change the outcome, *as it has already happened*.

As we have pointed out throughout *The Anger Fallacy*, anger simply interferes with solving the problems that you have to face in these situations. Each time you experience anger in a situation beyond your control, we want you to record it. Keep adding such experiences in a growing list in this section so that you can see how common your 'pointless' anger is. Don't stop until you find 20 examples in your own life. Oh, and don't forget to record the full details of these incidents (including the intensity of your anger) in you're Anger Diary (Exercise 1).

Example 1 _____

_____

Example 2 _____

_____

Example 3 _____

_____

Example 4 _____

_____

Example 5 _____

_____

Example 6 _____

_____

Example 7 _____

_____

Example 8 _____

_____

Example 9 _____

_____

Example 10 _____

_____

Example 11 _____

_____

Example 12 _____

_____

Example 13 _____

_____

Example 14 _____

_____

Example 15 _____

_____

Example 16 _____

_____

Example 17 _____

_____

Example 18 _____

_____

Example 19 _____

_____

Example 20 _____

_____

Mindfulness and Anger
— Living in the Moment

One of the reasons people get angry is that they stop 'living in the moment'. The next time you are standing in a queue, or held up in traffic, or in any other frustrating situation that is not actually painful, try to recognise that you are not really 'waiting' or 'being stood up' or 'in the wrong hotel room'. You are living in a series of moments in which you can experience any number of pleasant or neutral internal and external stimuli of your choosing. Focus on each of those moments and see how this affects your experience. Here is Michael's attempt while waiting in a local delicatessen:

> I entered the deli and had to take a numbered ticket. My number was 109, and I could see that they were only up to number 88. The shop was packed with people. I admit that I heard several 'angry sentences' arising in my consciousness: 'How long is this going to take!', 'They should have more staff on this counter', and 'This is bloody ridiculous'. But then I remembered my anger management lessons — I am only in a queue in my mind. I am continuing to live in a series of sensory moments. I am not waiting. I began to look at the different cheeses behind the glass. I focused on the blue-purple mould on the blues, and the various colours of the rinds on the hard cheeses. I moved my attention to the amalgam of smells that I had not noticed before. The tincture of burnt coffee and the forest floor odours of ripened cheese and cured meats combined. I wondered if anyone had ever experienced that precise combination of smells. I listened to the screams of the machine that cut the salami and watched it fall, slice by slice. Suddenly, I heard my number called.

In the following spaces, record your own attempts to 'live in the moment'.

Attempt 1

_____

_____

_____

_____

_____

Attempt 2

_____

_____

_____

_____

Attempt 3

_____

_____

_____

_____

_____

Attempt 4

_____

_____

_____

_____

_____

Attempt 5

_____

_____

_____

_____

_____

Does the Scene Really Matter?
Using the Memoirs Test

One of the most common problems in everyday experiences of anger is that the intensity of the emotion far outweighs the objective costs of the scene. That is, all too often anger is far in excess of the real importance or significance of the triggering event. Most moments of anger are over extremely trivial matters. Someone has run late for a meeting. A friend hasn't returned your call. The bank hasn't sent you your regular statement. The shop has sold out of the item you wanted. Your partner hasn't put his dirty shirt in the laundry basket.

In future, we want you to use the following simple test to help you decide whether the magnitude of your anger seems appropriate: If you were writing your autobiography, or the story of your life, would the current focus of your anger get a mention in the pages of this book? That is, would today's traffic jam really warrant a sentence or a paragraph in your memoirs? Would you really include any discussion of the fact that your local restaurant forgot the calamari in their last delivery to you?

We want you to use this 'memoirs test' in each new situation in which you feel anger arise. We argue that any incident that doesn't warrant a sentence or a footnote in an autobiography or memoir simply doesn't warrant anger. The incident is clearly too trivial.

Below, list 10 angry moments from your past that wouldn't pass the 'memoirs test'.

1. _____

_____

2. _____

_____

3. _____

_____

4. _____

_____

5. _____

_____

6. _____

_____

7. _____

_____

8. _____

_____

9. _____

_____

10. _____

_____

Now, moving forward, look out for new moments of anger that wouldn't pass the 'memoirs test'. Record 20 such moments over the coming months. Make sure that you also record the full details of these moments in your Anger Diary (Exercise 1).

1. _____

_____

2. _____

_____

3. _____

_____

4. _____

_____

5. _____

_____

6. _____

_____

7. _____

_____

8. _____

_____

9. _____

_____

10. _____

_____

11. _____

_____

12. _____

_____

13. _____

_____

14. _____

_____

15. _____

_____

16. _____

_____

17. _____

_____

18. _____

_____

19. _____

_____

20. _____

_____

Using a Responsibility Pie

Anger may arise because we oversimplify the causes of an event. We tend to blame a single individual for a negative outcome, even though there may be a multitude of contributing factors behind the event. This is called the *fallacy of the single cause.*

For example, Toby comes home from work to discover that his wife Julie has not been to the chemist and picked up his prescription medication as requested. He screams at Julie, believing that it is entirely her fault. However, his analysis is too simplistic. The following contributing factors show the circumstances that led to Julie's failure to get to the chemist:

- Toby had also asked her to get to the bank.
- Their bank branch is quite far from the chemist where Toby has an account.
- His mother rang to say she was coming over that evening. Julie had to shop to make dinner.
- Their youngest child (11 months) was sick that morning — she vomited and Julie put her back to bed.
- Their 3 year old, Michael, still needs a day sleep. Julie's main chance to go the bank was lost because Michael slept from 1pm to 4 pm that day.
- Julie rang the chemist at 4.30pm to get the prescription delivered, but she was told that deliveries stop at 4pm.
- Toby only mentioned his need for the prescription that morning. Had he not waited until he was all out of medication, the task would have been considerably easier.

Toby treats his wife as if she's lazy or inconsiderate, but shows little understanding of the complexity of her day. He also fails to consider his own contribution to the problem. Anger often arises when we fail to consider all the factors that have led to an event.

Record Your Reactions to a Situation

In the following exercise, we want you to use an example in which you believe you have been guilty of a similar mistake. That is, record an occasion when you blamed a single person for a bad outcome, when there was actually a range of contributing factors.

Situation 1

Provide the details of the occasion:

_____

_____

_____

List all the people *other* than the person you have blamed (including yourself) who have contributed to the bad outcome. Also, list any other circumstances that may have played a role in causing the outcome. When you have exhausted all the other people and circumstances that may have played a role, in last place, add the name of the person you originally blamed.

1._____ 6._____ 11._____

2._____ 7._____ 12._____

3._____ 8._____ 13._____

4._____ 9._____ 14._____

5._____ 10._____ 15._____

Now divide up the pie on the next page into slices, one for each person or circumstance that would have played a role in causing the negative outcome. Start with number 1 on your list, and continue until everyone (and every circumstance) on the list is given a piece of pie. Save the biggest pieces for the people or circumstances that you think would have played the greatest role in the event; the bigger the piece, the bigger the responsibility or causal role; the smaller the piece, the smaller the responsibility or causal role.

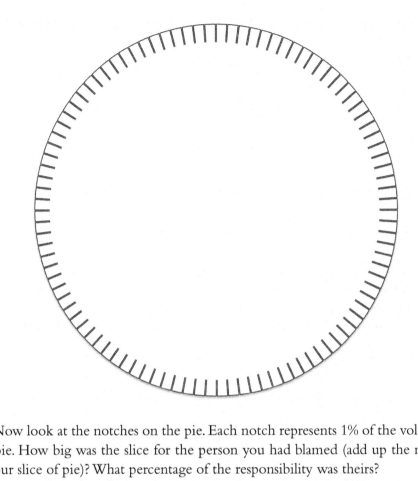

Now look at the notches on the pie. Each notch represents 1% of the volume of the pie. How big was the slice for the person you had blamed (add up the notches in your slice of pie)? What percentage of the responsibility was theirs?

_____

What have you learned about their responsibility for the negative outcome? Were they as responsible for the outcome as you previously thought?

_____

_____

_____

_____

_____

Now because we think this is such an important exercise, we want you to complete it two more times. Going over the complexities of situations in which you have felt anger toward an individual could really help you.

Situation 2

Provide the details of the occasion:

_____

_____

_____

As before, list all the people (other than the person you have blamed) who could have contributed to the bad outcome. List any other circumstances that may have played a role in causing the outcome. When you have exhausted all the other people and circumstances that may have played a role, add the name of the person you blamed last.

1. _____   6. _____   11. _____

2. _____   7. _____   12. _____

3. _____   8. _____   13. _____

4. _____   9. _____   14. _____

5. _____   10. _____   15. _____

Now divide up the pie on the next page into slices, one for each person or circumstance that would have played a role in causing the negative outcome. Start with number 1 on your list, and continue until everyone (and every circumstance) on the list is given a piece of pie. Remember, save the biggest pieces for the people or circumstances that you think would have played the greatest role in the event.

Remember each notch represents 1% of the volume of the pie. How big was the slice for the person you had blamed (add up the notches in your slice of pie)? What percentage of the responsibility was theirs? _____

What have you learned about their responsibility for the negative outcome? Were they as responsible for the outcome as you previously thought?

_____

_____

_____

_____

_____

And now, let's do this exercise again on another situation.

Situation 3

Provide the details of the occasion:

_____

_____

_____

_____

List all the people, circumstances and factors that could have contributed to the bad or annoying outcome. Add the name of the person you blamed last.

1._____   6._____   11._____

2._____   7._____   12._____

3._____   8._____   13._____

4._____   9._____   14._____

5._____   10._____   15._____

Now divide up the pie below into slices as you did before. Remember, the bigger the piece, the bigger the responsibility or causal role; the smaller the piece, the smaller the responsibility or causal role.

Now look at the notches on the pie. According to your own estimates, what percentage of the responsibility was theirs? _____

What have you learned about their responsibility for the negative outcome? Were they as responsible for the outcome as you previously thought?

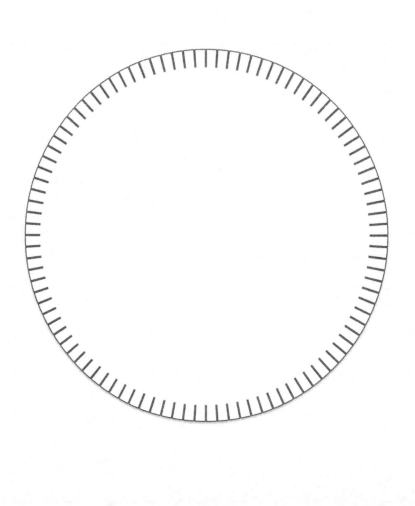

_____

_____

_____

_____

Now that you have completed three pie analyses, what have you learned about responsibility? Do you think there are ever really single causes for bad outcomes? Discuss:

_____

_____

_____

_____

_____

Change Your Attempts to Influence Those Around You

Often, anger in relationships arises on a weekly or daily basis, over the *same* issues, for many years. Renowned relationships expert john Gottman calls these 'gridlocked issues', but the common phrases 'bashing your head against a brick wall' and 'playing a broken record' come to mind too. Kristie has been angry with her husband over his lack of sexual interest for more than five years. Liam has fought with Stephanie over her untidiness for a decade. Despite the failure of angry displays to impact on core relationship issues, many of us just keep getting angry. Some believe it is the definition of insanity to do the same thing over and over and expect different results; stubbornness or stupidity seem to us credible alternatives. Perhaps it is time to accept the uselessness of anger as a strategy in producing change in the people around you. Below are 10 strategies that might have a greater impact on the situation.

1. Write a **letter** or email expressing how you feel about the issue and how important it is to you.

2. Come up with a **negotiation** plan — a tit-for-tat — in which you'll give something in return for your partner changing the behaviour you're concerned about. Use your imagination to come up with a range of offerings in exchange for the change in your partner's behaviour.

3. **Problem-solve** creatively. Actively and positively contribute to finding solutions to the problem (suggest moving the laundry basket to where Steven drops his clothes, get a cleaner in [using his credit card], draw up a roster, etc.).

4. Express **worry** or **sadness**, instead of anger, about the issue. They can be more poignant, and less likely to elicit defensiveness: 'Honey, I'm worried about your health (instead of, 'You eat like a pig!'); 'you know, I've been sad about us recently … What happened?'; 'Baby, when you speak to me like that I get scared. Scared about where we're going …'; 'I worry about the time you spend at work, and it really upsets me to hear the kids at bedtime asking, "when's daddy getting home?" etc.

5. Be **business-like** about the matter. Suggest that the two of you have a 'meeting'; that you prepare points for discussion, take minutes, draw up a plan of action, and resolve the issue in a very neutral, 'serious' manner.

6. Get **sentimental** instead of critical. Bring out the photos, the souvenirs. Talk about the times when your partner DID the things you reproach him for not doing: 'I loved it when you used to surprise me at work …'; 'I miss our walks …'; 'Remember this beach?'. Then just let it percolate.

7. Change the **setting** for the conversation. Take your partner out to dinner, and then reveal that the purpose of the meal is to discuss the matter calmly. Choose somewhere formal and/or public.

8. Seek his/her permission to get a **friend** or trusted colleague to discuss the issue with them.

9. Suggest that the two of you see a counsellor, psychologist, or other trained **mediator** to help solve the dilemma.

10. Change your **perspective**. Use the empathy solution (see chapter 10 of *The Anger Fallacy*) to be more accepting of the other person's point of view.

Each of these strategies is more likely to have an impact on your partner's behaviour because, if nothing else, they are. *novel* in the relationship. What is the point in having *another* fight over the issue when hundreds of previous fights have failed to resolve the matter?

Pick an Issue

We want you to pick an issue that regularly causes disputes in a pivotal relationship in your life. (This could be with a partner, parent, child or any significant other.) Then choose one of the 10 strategies listed earlier in this exercise and put it into action. Choose whichever strategy you believe will have the greatest chance of having an impact on the ongoing conflict. Record the results of your altered attempts to influence the situation in the following space.

_____

_____

_____

_____

_____

If your first attempt to have a positive impact on the situation fails, don't be surprised. As we pointed out in *The Anger Fallacy*, behavioural patterns develop over thousands of hours and are difficult to shift. And don't forget that the goal of this exercise is not necessarily *just* to change the other person's behaviour. The goal is to have *any* positive impact on the situation. This could mean less conflict, more empathy, a growing sense of cooperation or positivity in the relationship, or simply achieving improvement in the way you communicate. Did any of these results occur from your first attempt at this task?

_____

_____

_____

_____

If you were unsuccessful with your first choice from the list, we suggest you choose another option and try again. And we urge you to carefully consider the last (but not least) option. Is it time to change your perspective on the other person's behaviour? Is it truly the crime that you have made it out to be, or is it a more minor issue? Would it pass the memoirs test (see Exercise 21)? Record your efforts and the results below.

_____

_____

_____

_____

You may choose to continue working through the list if the issue remains significant to you.

In Other People's Words

Explaining the ideas of influential thinkers in your own words will help you deepen your understanding of the key points in *The Anger Fallacy*. Try the following.

1. Explain, in your own words, the meaning of this little parable, from Smile's *Self-Help*: "As I was going to the hills," said he, "early one misty morning, I saw something moving on a mountain side, so strange-looking that I took it for a monster. When I came nearer to it I found it was a man. When I came up to him I found he was my brother."

_____

_____

_____

_____

_____

2. Kafka described war as a 'monstrous failure of imagination'. How do you understand this phrase, considering what was covered in the empathy chapter of *The Anger Fallacy*?

_____

_____

_____

_____

_____

3. 'Each person is the centre of his universe just as you are the centre of yours'. Explain how this phrase might work to temper someone's anger.

_____

_____

_____

_____

4. Nelson Mandella famously said 'To be free is not merely to cast off one's chains, but to live in a way that respects and enhances the freedom of others'. How is this quote consistent with the central ideas of _The Anger Fallacy_?

_____

_____

_____

_____

5. Epictetus claimed that 'We have two ears and one mouth so that we can listen twice as much as we speak'. Why is listening so important if you are to conquer anger and conflict?

_____

_____

_____

_____

6. Discuss the wisdom in Plato's claim that 'there are two things a person should never be angry at: what they can help, and what they cannot'.

_____

_____

_____

_____

7. The American journalist Alexander Chase once wrote 'to understand is to forgive, even oneself". In your own words, explain his meaning.

_____

_____

_____

_____

8. The Dalai Lama said, 'If you learn to feel happy for other people's happiness, you increase your own chances of happiness 7 billion fold'. How is this relevant to your battle with anger?

_____

_____

_____

_____

_____

Getting Into the Skin of the Other Person

Most angry individuals *escalate* situations where they feel criticised or attacked. They try to defend themselves by increasing the volume of their voice, or making personal counterattacks, forcefully justifying themselves, and refusing to see (or at least openly acknowledge) the other person's perspective.

In the following exercises, we're going to encourage you to practise expressing how the other person involved in the conflict is feeling before launching into explanations or defensiveness. Rather than defend your own behaviour or perspective, try *first* to get into the skin of the other person. Here's a worked example to show you what we mean.

Example

Mary is twenty minutes late home from work and her partner, Tim, is very upset when she walks in the door. "You could have rung!" he declares. How should Mary respond here? What do you think would happen if she responded with 'I lost track of time, Jesus, relax!'. We're suggesting you substitute the empathic response. In choosing Mary's words, don't defend her actions in any way until *after* you've expressed Tim's perspective.

Suggested Response: "I'm sorry for not calling, sweetie. I know it must have been annoying. You've cooked for the two of us and I didn't even let you know I'd be late. You probably feel ignored. I imagine you felt increasingly frustrated as the minutes rolled on, particularly as the dinner was slowly going cold! You were probably thinking, 'why do I bother?' I am truly sorry — I just completely lost track of time. I'll set the alarm on my phone for 4 pm in future. That way I can call you one hour before I'm due home to confirm if all is going well or let you know if I'm running late'."

Authors' Comment: Notice how Mary's empathic response was followed by an explanation and a possible solution for the future. The more you get into the skin of the people around you, the more you will genuinely feel their pain and seek to redress any hurt that they have felt. Empathy is a first step to finding behavioural solutions to everyday problems. More cynically, it serves a diplomatic and strategic function; if you don't acknowledge their harm they won't listen to your reasons or solutions, and they will harbour resentment. So here are four examples for you to complete.

Situation 1

You'd promised to take your 12-year-old son to the skate park after school but forgot you'd made an appointment for him with the dentist. You tell him when you pick him up at school and he responds with venom. 'Typical — you never keep your promises to me'. Respond, by 'living in the skin of the other person'. That is, try to express how you think the boy is feeling. In choosing the father's words, don't defend his actions in any way until *after* you've expressed the child's perspective.

_____

_____

_____

_____

_____

Situation 2

You are working at an international airport for a major airline. You have just announced that a flight has been cancelled due to technical difficulties with the plane and now have to deal with angry customers. The first man approaches spitting his words out, 'I've GOT to get to Paris NOW! I mean, this is outrageous! Do you guys even bother to maintain your planes? Some of us actually have schedules that we need to keep.

Respond by 'living in the skin of the other person". That is, try to express how you think the businessman is feeling. In choosing the staff member's words, don't defend the airline in any way until *after* you've expressed the customer's perspective.

_____

_____

_____

_____

_____

_____

Situation 3

You put your lover's favourite champagne flutes in the dishwasher and it ruins the gold leaf trim on each of them. They were a present from her mother who has now passed away. You show her the glasses and she explodes saying 'are you a fucking idiot? How could you have done this? You don't give a fuck about my things!'. She storms off to the bedroom and is crying. After a few minutes, you go to her.

Now try to 'live in the skin of the other person'. That is, try to express how you think she is feeling. In choosing your words, don't defend yourself in any way until *after* you've expressed her perspective.

_____

_____

_____

_____

Situation 4

Your partner approaches you for sex. You are not really in the mood and you roll away from his touch saying, 'I'm very tired'. He explodes, and says 'You're not tired at all — you just don't care about me or how I feel, and you never have!'

Now try to live in the skin of the other person. That is, try to express how you think he is feeling in reaction to your response. In choosing the wife's words, don't defend her in any way until *after* you've expressed her partner's perspective.

_____

_____

_____

_____

_____

Having practised 'getting in the skin of the other person' in these situations, we want you to try this style of communication when you find yourself in scenes involving possible conflict.

Record Your Communication Attempts

Over the coming weeks, record five attempts to communicate by first stating the other person's perspective, and then attempting to communicate effectively without anger.

Attempt 1 _____

_____

_____

_____

Attempt 2 _____

_____

_____

_____

_____

Attempt 3 _____

_____

_____

_____

Attempt 4 _____

_____

_____

_____

Attempt 5 _____

_____

_____

_____

This style of communication is difficult at first. It may seem unnatural or forced. But with practice you will form new communication habits that will reduce conflict and, perhaps more importantly, help you to conquer your own anger.

Compassion Visualisation

Try the following Buddhist visualisation:

- Sit somewhere calmly, breathing slowly. Imagine something soothing and reassuring. This can be a 'safe place' or happy memory, or the Buddhist suggestion of the 'perfect nurturer', the compassionate Buddha or some such thing flowing into you like warm light.

- When you feel calm, bring to mind your own struggles and pain; acknowledge it hasn't been easy but that you've done your best; 'try on' the feeling of total acceptance and peace; cock a half smile; and feel warm sympathy for your suffering, as if looking upon yourself as an old friend.

- Say (to yourself): 'I hope you can find relief from your suffering, my friend'.

- Now do the same for a loved one: imagine their suffering; acknowledge their efforts and struggles, and say: 'I hope you can find relief from your suffering, my friend'.

- Now do the same for a relatively neutral acquaintance (e.g., a colleague or neighbour) for whom you have no strong feelings, positive or negative.

- Now do the same for a person you dislike, or for a rival.

- If it is too difficult or disingenuous for you to wish this person well, imagine looking them in the face and saying, 'You and I have not always seen eye to eye. I'm sorry this is the case, because essentially we're the same, and in different circumstances might have been allies or friends.'

- Observe how this changes your day. If you find this a useful exercise, we recommend you practising it for a few minutes every day. The positive effects on your wellbeing can be striking.

Practising Patience

Many Buddhist practices focus on displaying patience and compassion, and labeling behaviours accordingly before performing them. In our clinical experience, such practices are a useful way of learning to overcome anger in everyday situations in which frustration arises. We want you to explore patience and compassion in the following experiment.

Visit a local delicatessen (or similar business) with the intention of letting someone be served before you. That is, you are going to let someone 'jump the queue'. You need to rehearse the following sentence in your mind just before entering the shop: 'By this act of patience and compassion for my fellow traveller, I will gain contentment'.

At the counter, let another customer gain the attention of the shop assistant before you, even though it is your turn. If necessary, gesture to the other shopper, saying, 'You can order — I'm still thinking'.

Response(s) to Practising Patience

How do you normally behave in these situations? How would you normally react if someone were served before their turn?

_____

_____

_____

_____

_____

Was it difficult to be patient?

_____

_____

_____

_____

How did the other shopper/s react to your patience, if at all?

_____

_____

_____

_____

How did you feel during the task?

_____

_____

_____

_____

What benefits do you think you would get if you continued to practise patience and compassion in this way?

_____

_____

_____

_____

_____

Now, we want you to practise this type of patience and compassion at least once every week for the coming 8 weeks. You can vary the scenes of course, but each should involve you purposefully putting other people before you. And remember, label your intention before each scene with the following words: 'By this act of patience and compassion for my fellow traveller, I will gain contentment'. Record the details of each of you attempts at patience and compassion.

Situation I

Describe the situation.

_____

_____

Was it difficult to be patient?

_____

_____

_____

How did the other individual/s react to your patience, if at all?

_____

_____

_____

How did you feel during the task?

_____

_____

_____

Situation 2

Describe the situation.

_____

_____

Was it difficult to be patient?

_____

_____

_____

How did the other individual/s react to your patience, if at all?

_____

_____

_____

How did you feel during the task?

_____

_____

_____

Situation 3

Describe the situation.

_____

_____

Was it difficult to be patient?

_____

_____

_____

How did the other individual/s react to your patience, if at all?

_____

_____

_____

How did you feel during the task?

_____

_____

_____

Situation 4

Describe the situation.

_____

_____

Was it difficult to be patient?

_____

_____

_____

How did the other individual/s react to your patience, if at all?

_____

_____

_____

How did you feel during the task?

_____

_____

_____

Situation 5

Describe the situation.

_____

_____

Was it difficult to be patient?

_____

_____

_____

How did the other individual/s react to your patience, if at all?

_____

_____

_____

How did you feel during the task?

_____

_____

_____

Situation 6

Describe the situation.

_____

_____

Was it difficult to be patient?

_____

_____

_____

How did the other individual/s react to your patience, if at all?

_____

_____

_____

How did you feel during the task?

_____

_____

_____

Situation 7

Describe the situation.

_____

_____

Was it difficult to be patient?

_____

_____

_____

How did the other individual/s react to your patience, if at all?

_____

_____

_____

How did you feel during the task?

_____

_____

_____

Situation 8

Describe the situation.

_____

_____

Was it difficult to be patient?

_____

_____

_____

How did the other individual/s react to your patience, if at all?

_____

_____

_____

How did you feel during the task?

_____

_____

_____

Understanding Other People's Interests and Activities

Here are three short tasks to get you to flexibly move away from your own perspective.

Task I

Pick an activity that you find especially obnoxious or pointless and that you just don't *get* (e.g.. social media, cricket, collecting). Interview at least one dedicated fan as openly and empathically as possible in order to try to understand it. Remember, your goal is to move away from your own perspective, a little like an actor who might research a role very unlike himself.

What activity did you choose?

_____

_____

What were the key attractions of the activity, according to its proponents?

_____

_____

_____

Were you able to suspend your own negative preconceptions about the activity? If so, were you able to see the positives of the activity?

_____

_____

_____

_____

Task 2

Research any of the following subject areas: veganism; psychedelic drug use; polygamy; or high fashion. Choose whichever lifestyle you find strangest or most objectionable. Why do people partake in them? What are their perceived benefits? Plan a five-minute pitch as if your task was to 'sell' them as a way of life. Remember, your goal is to move away from your own perspective.

What were the key arguments that you raised in your speech?

_____

_____

_____

_____

_____

_____

Again, were you able to suspend your own negative preconceptions about the practice? If so, were you able to genuinely see the positives of the lifestyle that attract some people?

_____

_____

_____

_____

Task 3

Watch the television show you hate the most. When you feel irritated, try to focus your attention on what the show's most devoted viewers might enjoy about it. You can stop when and only when your irritation has abided and you can genuinely say, 'Alright, I suppose I get it ...'.

Write a short paragraph on what you think others like in the show.

_____

_____

_____

_____

_____

_____

_____

Identifying With Both Sides

Choose a film from the following list (or a favourite of your own, so long as it involves two people in conflict). We want you to get into the shoes of the two opposing characters listed.

- *Bladerunner* — Deckard vs. Roy
- *Meet the Fockers* — Father vs. Son-in-law
- *The Lion King* — Mufasa vs. Scar
- *Kramer vs. Kramer* — Ted vs. Joanna
- *Skyfall* — Raoul Silva vs. Bond
- *Raiders of the Lost Ark* — Indiana Jones vs. Dr Rene Belloq
- or a film of your choice.

Now, write a paragraph explaining the perspective of each of the two rivals. Can you defend them both? Can you view both characters as neither 'right' nor 'wrong'?

Character 1:_____

_____

_____

_____

_____

_____

Character 2:_____

_____

_____

_____

_____

Now let's do it again. Choose another film and complete the same task. Each time you get in the skin of opposing characters it will help your empathy skills which will, in turn, help you master anger.

Character 1:_____

_____

_____

_____

_____

Character 2:_____

_____

_____

_____

And one more time. Choose a third film and complete the same task.

Character 1:_____

_____

_____

_____

_____

Character 2:_____

_____

_____

_____

_____

The Egocentricity of Anger

To complete this exercise you will first need to watch Episode 5 in Series 1 of the television show *Curb Your Enthusiasm*. The episode, 'Interior Designer', focuses on a range of angry moments in the life of Larry David. It is a hilarious study on the self-ishness and pointlessness of anger.

Anger Scenarios and Your Responses

Larry is initially angry about the waiting room policy at his doctor's practice. What is the policy and what change does Larry suggest?

_____

_____

_____

What does he do to express his frustration over having to wait? Does it help his situation at all?

_____

_____

_____

The woman in front of him spends 45 minutes with the doctor. When she emerges from the doctor's office how does Larry deal with her? Does he appear compassionate towards the woman?

_____

_____

_____

He claims that the woman wouldn't let him pass her in the hall. Do you think this was true?

_____

_____

_____

He appears angry with the other patients in the waiting room for not offering him support in his plight. Can you express his anger as a 'should' statement?

_____

_____

_____

Larry asks the doctor to change his 'ridiculous' waiting room policy. However, when the change is made, he becomes angry. Why?

_____

_____

_____

The lawyer is angry in the episode. Express one or more of these moments as 'should' statements.

_____

_____

_____

The doctor is angry in the episode. Express one or more of these moments as 'should' statements.

_____

_____

_____

The doctor's administrative assistant is angry in the episode. Express one or more of these moments as 'should' statements.

_____

_____

_____

The parking attendant is angry in the episode. Express one or more of these moments as 'should' statements.

_____

_____

_____

The interior designer is angry in the episode. Express one or more of these moments as 'should' statements.

_____

_____

_____

Diane Keaton is, we are told, angry in the episode. Express one or more of these moments as 'should' statements.

_____

_____

_____

How many people does Larry assault in the episode?

_____

_____

_____

Does Larry's anger achieve anything in the episode?

_____

_____

_____

Does Larry's anger cost him anything in the episode?

_____

_____

_____

The episode is summed up when Larry declares that the policy should be 'me first'. He nods at the administrative assistant and declares 'Me first! That's the policy!'. What does this statement teach you about the nature of anger?

_____

_____

_____

_____

_____

_____

Anger as Frustrated Craving

As you could see in the previous exercise, anger is often a very selfish emotion. It tends to arise when our own desires have been delayed or ignored. Another ancient piece of Buddhist thinking suggests that anger is often simply 'frustrated craving', where 'craving' here means any kind of desire, goal, attachment or need. The two-year-old boy hits you and screams because you are not rewarding his craving for another chocolate. He perceives you as the roadblock to his goal. The queue is too long at the bank today and you are in a hurry. The bank is frustrating your desire to get home and you are angry. Your internet connection keeps dropping out and you are angry. The internet service provider is interfering with your wish for concert tickets. Your children are playing noisily in the family room when you are craving peace and quiet and so you explode. Your wife rejects your sexual advances and you are very angry — your craving for sexual gratification will not be rewarded tonight and you target your anger at the perceived cause of your frustration.

It might be disconcerting to have your anger outbursts compared to a 2-year-old's selfish clamouring for another chocolate, but do you really think the comparison is unreasonable? If you're honest with yourself we believe that you will be able to identify frustrated craving at the heart of most of your anger.

Record 20 examples of frustrated cravings leading to anger over the days and weeks ahead. They shouldn't be hard to find.

1. _____

_____

2. _____

_____

3. _____

_____

4. _____

_____

5. _____

_____

6. _____

_____

7. _____

_____

8. _____

_____

9. _____

_____

10. _____

_____

11. _____

_____

12. _____

_____

13. _____

_____

14. _____

_____

15. _____

_____

16. _____

_____

17. _____

_____

18. _____

_____

19. _____

_____

20. _____

Being Servile for One Hour

As we have said, anger can be a very selfish emotion. It arises because you are putting yourself ahead of others. Your desires, your opinions, your beliefs *must be served*! In these contexts, the angry person is essentially displaying 'feelings of entitlement'. Because of this, anyone with a history of anger can benefit from the equal and opposite practice of serving the needs of others. Humility and self-sacrifice is the antidote to entitlement. We want you to serve those around you for just one hour and record the results on your mood, anger levels, and general demeanour. Serve in the way a doting grandparent might respond to the first-born grandchild that they have waited so long for.

Examples

The following response to this task is from Stan, an angry 48-year-old administrative assistant:

> I attempted this task on a Friday evening. When I arrived home I remarked that my wife looked tired and asked her if she would like to sit down and rest. I brought her a cup of tea and her favourite magazine. I put a load of washing on and asked the children if they would like me to read to them. My 6-year-old daughter was excited but my 10 year old just shrugged. I asked him what he would like to do and he wanted me to play chess. I agreed to a game after reading to my daughter and both were very happy. I got down on the floor (something I rarely do) with my 3-year-old to play with his toy cars. The hour quickly turned into two and I was very happy. And my family all seemed very happy. Resentment, at least for that evening, had washed away and I felt more connected than I had in a long time.

And this response is from Mary, a 41-year-old doctor:

Serve?? That's all I bloody do!! Serve the needs of my patients, my children or my selfish husband. But OK, I'll try it. I walked in the house and saw toys and mess everywhere. I started to get angry and remembered the task. Why shouldn't the toys be out? The children play with them. It's what they like. (ASIDE: I realise that my anger toward children around mess is simply my 'frustrated craving' for tidiness). To my surprise, I heard myself ask the children if they would like me to join them in play. They were delighted. We made more mess and I enjoyed the game. They were very loud, but I didn't get angry (though I normally would). Children like to be loud, and I was serving their needs for this hour. At times they fought, but I didn't get angry. Siblings often fight and I smiled and tried to smooth things over (like I know their grandmother would). They asked if we could go out for dinner and I (reluctantly) agreed. I was tired and wanted to reheat leftovers but they wanted sushi. So we went and I held their hands as we walked. I asked them what they would like to talk about and all they wanted to do was plan a fun weekend. So we did, with their desires and aspirations at the centre of all the plans. I have to admit, I had a great night and was anger-free throughout.

OK, now it's your turn. Remember, for one hour you are to serve others around you. It can be at home, or at work, or out with friends. It doesn't really matter. What counts is that you serve with a loving, patient heart. Record your results below. What happened to your mood, anger levels and general functioning?

_____

_____

_____

_____

_____

_____

_____

_____

Record Your Experiences Over Seven Weeks

We think this task is so important that we want you do it at least once a week over the next seven weeks. It will really help overcome any feelings of 'entitlement', which will in turn reduce your anger.

Detail your experience of serving others for one hour.

Week 1 _____

_____

_____

_____

_____

_____

_____

_____

Week 2 _____

_____

_____

_____

_____

_____

_____

_____

_____

_____

Week 3_____

_____

_____

_____

_____

_____

_____

_____

Week 4_____

_____

_____

_____

_____

_____

_____

_____

_____

Week 5_____

_____

_____

_____

_____

_____

_____

_____

Week 6_____

_____

_____

_____

_____

_____

_____

_____

_____

_____

Week 7_____

_____

_____

_____

_____

_____

_____

_____

See Miscreants as Fascinating or Humorous Machines

Chapter 9 of *The Anger Fallacy*, 'Seeing the machine', discusses the way in which the human brain is essentially an organic machine — a supercomputer — and not just metaphorically. The decisions that people around you make, and the often undesirable behaviour that follows, are essentially the result of the firing of neurons in their brains, which in turn are configured and programmed the way they are because of a combination of their biology and biography.

There are a number of well-known robots from film or television: Astro Boy; the Jetsons' household robot Rosie; HAL from *2001: A Space Odyssey*; C–3PO and R2-D2 from *Star Wars*; and of course the *Terminator*. These robots have featured all manner of personality and motivation, fully equipped with quirks and idiosyncrasies, some lovable, some terrifying. It's no stretch at all to see them as being much like people, but for some reason it's much harder to see people as being much like robots. That, however, is what we are asking you to try here.

Your task is to choose a few people who frequently annoy you and to see them as organic machines—and to label them as such. Read the examples, below, and complete the following task.

Examples

Uncle Jack: 'Grumpy old man cyborg, model 1949, running stingy aspy curmudgeon software, 4th edition'.

Niece Sasha: 'Entitled teenage girl cyborg, model 2000, running 'whatever' and 'talk to the hand' loop tapes'.

Stressed boss: 'Smoking, overweight worried businessman cyborg, model 1955, running "DO IT NOW" frowning software through gritted, yellowed teeth'.

Your Task

Can you label five people who occasionally annoy you in a similar fashion?

1. _____

2. _____

3. _____

4. _____

5. _____

When you next encounter these individuals, remind yourself of the humorous 'machine label' that you've given them. And don't forget that there's truth behind the label (i.e., humans are electrical machines programmed by biology and biography). Do you really think it's reasonable to blame a machine for its hardware and software?

_____

Look After the State of Your Organism

All other things being equal, the *state* you're in as you enter an anger-provoking scene will influence the likelihood and severity of an angry reaction. If you are stressed, tired, ill, hung-over, agitated, or in an emotionally compromised state when you encounter a provocation, then you are more likely to fall back on old, unreflected patterns of responding — more likely to overreact.

The following are the four key variables of interest. Your task here is to do something towards reducing the levels of each category.

Drugs/alcohol/stimulants

Drug and alcohol abuse is the most common co-morbid condition of patients presenting with anger problems. Alcohol reduces self-control; stimulants boost arousal levels (including caffeine and nicotine if you're not used to them). And just about any recreational drug will have an aversive rebound effect of some kind or another — a 'come down' — which will leave you susceptible.

What I have done to reduce or minimise my use of drugs/alcohol/stimulants:

_____

_____

_____

_____

_____

_____

Tiredness

Tiredness is a double whammy: it makes you more likely to react angrily to a situation, and less able to think your way out of it. Poor sleep is the usual cause, but there are many others: health, diet, exercise, and sunlight all contribute.

What I have done towards feeling better rested in the day:

_____

_____

_____

_____

_____

Burnout

Long periods of intense concentration or inhibition (such as you might experience at work or with the in-laws) will tax you and deplete your self-control. Self-control, as it turns out, is like a muscle, and can get fatigued if not allowed some respite during the day. *Overworking* is the prime suspect here.

What I have done towards feeling less taxed or overworked:

_____

_____

_____

_____

_____

_____

Any aversive or arousal state

This could be unmet needs (e.g., hunger, thirst, discomfort, lust); sickness; a negative emotional state such as stress, anxiety, sadness, and so on.

What I have done towards feeling generally better and more comfortable:

_____

_____

_____

_____

_____

Reducing background variables is a good, easy start in the fight against anger. Get some sleep, take some time off, streamline your week, delegate, relax, improve your diet, and so on. But remember these variables are neither necessary nor sufficient to cause anger, and so we don't want you blaming them too much for your angry tendencies!

Who Do You Wish to Become?

All of the exercises in this workbook, in one way or another, have focused on reinventing the way in which you react to difficulties in life. In this final task, we want you to sum up your aspirations for your 'future self'. Who do you wish to become over the years ahead? How do you wish to behave during your remaining years on this planet? Try to visualise your best possible self in a way that is positive for you. Be sure to write down the character strengths that you want in your future. You might choose to describe the reactions of someone close to you that you admire. Trying to emulate or mirror the reactions of a calm friend, family member or colleague can be a positive way forward in your battle with anger. And feel free to reference characters from film or television whose reactions you respect. Perhaps they have qualities that you want in your future.

There is no right or wrong response to this exercise. Just take your time, and think about the core issue: How do you wish to deal with your fellow man in the future? Who do you want to be?

Verbal Cues … chilled, tolerant, an example, self-controlled, easy-going, wise, forgiving, compassionate, even-tempered, fun, friendly, loving, kind, warm, cool, relaxed, calm, light-hearted.

Context cues … How do you wish to react in the following contexts:

At work

_____

_____

_____

_____

_____

_____

With children

_____

_____

_____

_____

_____

With friends

_____

_____

_____

_____

_____

_____

_____

With strangers

_____

_____

_____

_____

_____

In moments of personal frustration

_____

_____

_____

_____

_____

We suggest that you re-read these descriptions at least once a week as you continue to work on your anger problems over the months ahead. Regularly reminding yourself of who you're wanting to become, will help you move toward your target self.

CPSIA information can be obtained
at www.ICGtesting.com
Printed in the USA
LVOW03s1551190416

484332LV00008B/174/P

9 781922 117373